Contents

Introduction 6
Acknowledgements 8
Dedication 10
Knowing When Your Child is Ready 11
Finding the Best Teacher for You 23
Place and Space Contribute to Success 37
I am CEO of My Business 49
Practice Guidelines that have Proven Successful 61
Want to Please Your Teacher? Practice! 73
Overcoming Challenges Presented in Music Lessons 87
Lights! Camera! Action! Pursue Performance Opportunities 95
How Parents can be Super Supportive 105
Words of Wisdom to the Teacher 115
Citations 126
Resources 127
About the Six-Word Lessons Series 128

Introduction

I have wanted, on many occasions, to gather the parents of my students and parents of my colleague's students, and discuss the ins and outs of what it takes to operate a successful private music instruction business. But because this would be impossible in this over-extended, time-consuming 21st century, I decided to write down everything I thought would help parents understand what I and my teaching colleagues do, and how parents can help enhance the relationships I have with them and their children. The culmination of that writing is this book. The Six-Word Lesson format is perfect for today's reader as it is to the point and the chapters of practical advice are short and quick to read, yet packed with valuable information.

Even though I am a piano and voice teacher, these lessons are designed for any and all music lesson students and parents, with the exception of Chapter 3, which has some specific lessons for those taking piano lessons.

It's always a risk to speak on behalf of an entire culture--private music instructors--but I hope all of the teachers who read this book will, at least one time, exclaim, "Yes, that is so true!" It's also a risk to call myself an "expert." My expertise lies solely in the

"This is the book I wish I could put into the hands of every parent of every music student in my studio!" - Sam Ecoff, former president, Wisconsin State Federation of Music Clubs, private music teacher, composer

"Reading this book was like sitting down and having a conversation with Sally, my colleague and friend." - Hallee Viniotis, president, Washington State Federation of Music Clubs, private teacher, accompanist

"I am the parent of a former student who excelled with Sally as a teacher. I found her writing style easy to read and implement. I believe she's the best in her industry!" - Kim Moger, parent of former student

"Sally Palmer has written a must-read primer for anyone considering music lessons...Read this book! - and learn from someone who knows the field inside and out." - Nancy Bos, international voice teacher, National Association of Teachers of Singing board member, and author of *Singing 101: Vocal Basics and Fundamental Singing Skills for All Styles and Abilities*

"A 'must read' for every parent who intends on giving their child music lessons of any kind. A great read for all independent music teachers, whether beginning their career or the well-seasoned teacher who needs a boost. Concise, polite but firm and informative for parents. It will now be part of my Parent Package as required reading prior to taking on any new student!" - Carol Champney, former president, Washington State Federation of Music Clubs, private music teacher

Six-Word Lessons for
EXCEPTIONAL MUSIC LESSONS

100 Lessons to Enhance the Parent, Teacher and Student Relationship

Sally L. Palmer

Published by Pacelli Publishing
Bellevue, Washington

Six-Word Lessons for Exceptional Music Lessons

All rights reserved. No part of this book may be reproduced or transmitted in any form or by any means, electronic or mechanical including photocopying, recording or by any information storage or retrieval system, without the written permission of the publisher, except where permitted by law.

Limit of Liability: While the author and the publisher have used their best efforts in preparing this book, they make no representation or warranties with respect to accuracy or completeness of the content of this book. The advice and strategies contained herein may not be suitable for your situation. Consult with a professional when appropriate.

Copyright © 2017 by Sally L. Palmer, All Rights Reserved

Published by Pacelli Publishing
9905 Lake Washington Blvd. NE, #D-103
Bellevue, Washington 98004
PacelliPublishing.com

ISBN-10: 1-933750-59-6
ISBN-13: 978-1-933750-59-0

almost 40 years of teaching, working with students of all ages and their parents. I've experienced a lot, I've read a lot, and I've learned incredibly valuable lessons through the years.

I believe that if every teacher could place this book in the hands of the parents of their students, the relationship between teachers and parents would truly be an exceptional experience, which ultimately will benefit your students.

So, consider yourself "gathered!" Now let's enjoy the discussion.

Acknowledgements

With deep gratitude, I would like to acknowledge all of the teachers in my life who have taught me great lessons in teaching. It's not just the words we use but how we present the words that has the greatest impact. I have been taught by great teachers.

I would like to thank my colleagues in the music teaching industry. We commiserate, we share, we uplift, and we laugh. This is not a job for the faint of heart or thin of skin, but a job to help us develop compassion and patience.

A special thank you to Wendy Stevens who helped me see that putting policies and procedures in place would make a big difference in my attitude about working. Wendy is a superhero in the business of teaching music. Another huge thank-you goes out to Nancy Bos who has taught me that it is never too late to make course corrections and take risks. Nancy uplifts my spirit. If these two people had not been placed in my life, this experience might never have happened.

This book would not have been possible if it weren't for Lonnie and Patty Pacelli of Pacelli Publishing. They actually approached me with this idea and then let me run with it, even though I was fearful of failure. Patty was extremely encouraging through the process and her faith in me kept me moving forward. She is a colleague, my editor and my publisher, but above all else, she is my dear friend.

Dedication

Dedicated to my Daddy, who believed I could do anything I put my heart and head into, and who loved listening to me play the piano.

Dedicated to my little sweet pea Eva, who brings sunshine into my life and keeps me young.

Knowing When Your Child is Ready

"If it wasn't hard, everyone would do it. It's the hard... that makes it great."

~ *A League of Their Own, 1992 film*

When can my child begin lessons?

Music teachers get asked this question all the time, and the answer is pretty much the same: when your child is ready is the best time to begin. Personally, I don't take children before the age of five, preferably six, for several reasons. Some teachers design their teaching programs specifically for kids younger than grade school.

2

My kid loves to play piano.

There is so much information on the Internet about how starting piano lessons early helps brain development in the young child, and research proves it to be so. That doesn't mean that if a preschooler walks up to a piano and starts plunking down on the keys he should immediately be signed up for piano lessons. Children under the age of five who show an interest in music can be exposed to many musical opportunities that don't require formal lessons.

Know the alphabet, right and left.

It is essential for a child starting music lessons to know the alphabet, especially the first seven letters, as they make up the music alphabet. It would be extra helpful to know those first seven letters forwards and backwards. Knowing the right hand from the left hand is also very useful for young beginners. Parents can help with these things at home.

Hand size, finger independence truly matters.

The best time for a child to begin piano lessons truly depends on the child. I prefer no earlier than six years old, but will certainly consult with parents of a five-year-old. During a consultation with a younger student, I will take a look at the child's hand size to see if her hands have grown enough to press down the keys with the fingers independent of each other.

Desire and interest of the child

During an interview with a young child, I speak directly to the child and see if I can gauge the level of desire and interest of the child (not the parent). If I can tell that a student isn't really interested in the piano but seems to have an interest in music, I will encourage the parent to look for musical opportunities other than piano lessons, and come back in a year.

Sitting with your child at practice.

Teachers, like me, who use book-based methods, need to know if a young student has good reading and understanding capabilities. If not, parents need to understand that they will need to be heavily involved in order for their child to progress. That involvement includes sitting with the child at home practice sessions. Parents, make sure you can commit to that level of involvement.

Attention span during practice and lessons

Attention span is another consideration with the very young starting music lessons. At the initial interview, expectations from both the parent and the teacher need to be openly discussed. A teacher may ask about the child's classroom experience in school. Can the child sit still during reading time? Teachers may need to adjust a teaching plan for a particular child to involve more activity during the lesson time.

Is it too late to learn?

Another question teachers get is, "Is it too late for me to learn?" This question usually comes from adults. The answer is NO. It may be easier to learn new skills when the brain is still developing, but that just means young adults and older adults may have to work a little harder. If the desire is there, it can be done. After all, hand and finger strength is no longer an issue!

When is it time to stop?

Parents should never force their children to take music lessons. I, personally, do not want to teach a child who is being forced to take lessons. It will cause a lot of contention in the home and in lessons. If a child who has been forced to take lessons eventually quits (which he will) he may never, ever yearn to play again. Keep the door open by not forcing your child through it to begin with.

Developing love of music through piano

Remember, music lessons are a lifetime investment. Students who continue their piano lessons through high school often consider the purchase of an instrument as an adult because they have developed musical skills and a love of music, which will continue to enrich their life and those around them.

Finding the Best Teacher for You

"A mediocre music teacher tells. A good music teacher explains. A superior music teacher demonstrates. A great music teacher inspires."

~ *William Arthur Ward, author*

11

As excitement mounts, find a teacher.

It's very exciting to begin music lessons for the first time! No matter the reason, whether it be that you, as the parent, took lessons years ago, or that you read somewhere that taking music lessons increases brain development, you are about to embark on a new adventure. You will find a variety of teacher personalities and teaching styles.

Does anyone have a good recommendation?

There are several music associations and organizations you can contact for teacher referrals and information. You can search for teachers in your geographic area as well as teachers who specialize in teaching young children, or those with disabilities, or adults. You can also do a little further research and look for teachers who specialize in theory development or competition preparation. Also, don't forget to ask your friends and neighbors for recommendations.

How to find the best teacher.

Your number one goal, as a parent, should be to make sure you find the right teacher for your student. A parent, teacher, student consultation or interview is a must before signing on the dotted line. This is an opportunity for questions to be asked of all three parties. Make sure goals and expectations line up. Observe to see if your child is comfortable in the presence of the teacher.

Go to interview prepared with questions.

Holding the initial interview in the teacher's music studio is a great way to discover if your child will feel comfortable in that particular environment. I invite the student to sit on the piano bench during the interview. It gives the prospective student an opportunity to play the piano, if he desires, and to get a feel for the room. Parents can see for themselves the teacher's environment, creativity and organization.

Take time to think it over.

Do not feel like you need to make an immediate decision about a teacher. If you feel a teacher is "the one" then go ahead and commit, but remember, the parent is the final decision maker. Don't feel bad about interviewing other teachers for comparison. When a parent and a child agree on a teacher that meets their needs, that is the time to make the commitment.

Make sure the student has time.

A word to the wise: over-scheduling a child is not helpful to anyone. Be careful about adding one more thing to an already busy child's agenda of activities. You may see that there is time once a week to schedule in a 45-minute music lesson, but remember, that means 45 minutes of practice each day also. Time management is critical.

Helping student over the proverbial wall

At some point in a music student's years of study, she may want to quit because "it's really hard." At the initial interview, parents should ask the teacher how he handles this situation. Parents can help by having their child make a commitment to the whole year of study to eliminate the opting out because it gets hard.

When playing can be considered therapeutic

Teenagers are prone to depression, exhaustion and frustration when they feel overwhelmed. Parents, talk to the prospective teacher about flexibility in assignments and performances. Talk to your child and find out their goals regarding music lessons during this stressful, hormonally-challenged chapter of their lives. Maybe the focus needs to shift to playing the instrument for therapy.

Studio policies on cancellations and rescheduling

During the interview period, ask the teacher about her flexibility, especially if your child is involved in year-round athletics. Make sure you understand the studio policy on cancellations and rescheduling. Some teachers use a "swap list" which is helpful when a student wants or needs to swap lessons with another student.

Student information form and enrollment contract

Once the decision has been made, the teacher should ask you to fill out a student information form. This gives the teacher your contact information and some additional information (such as allergies or challenges) about your child. Also at the time of commitment, the teacher may ask for you to sign an enrollment contract. Some teachers may even ask for a deposit or the first month's tuition.

Withholding critical information is not helpful.

It is very important to let a music teacher know if the student has any learning challenges or difficulties, such as dyslexia, autism, ADD, ADHD, or any auditory or verbal challenges. It is not fair to the student or the teacher if these issues are not addressed. Lessons and practice guidelines can be altered for children with these challenges. Some teachers are specially trained to teach children with various disabilities.

Make sure you read before signing.

The enrollment contract should specify that you have been informed of or have read the studio policies and procedures and that you commit to abiding by those policies and procedures. Make sure you thoroughly read the policies and procedures before you sign. Ask for a written copy of the policies so you can refer to them in the future when you have questions.

Place and Space Contribute to Success

"Good piano playing is only possible if we are comfortably seated at the piano."

~ *Dr. Teresa Dybvig,*
founder of "The Well-Balanced Pianist"

Is a piano needed at home?

When a student begins piano lessons, having a piano at home may seem obvious, but parents still ask, "Do I need to buy a piano?" While a keyboard is necessary, whether it be acoustic piano, weighted keys keyboard, or electronic keyboard, there are other options, especially for the young beginning student, if a parent does not want to make the acoustic piano investment quite yet. However, progress cannot be made without some type of keyboard.

Why does your piano sound different?

If you do have an acoustic piano, have it tuned! Besides the fact that regular tunings (twice a year) will keep your piano healthy for many years to come, a student will not arrive at the teacher's studio and exclaim, "Your piano sounds so different than mine!" Students with keen hearing can be thrown off by the sound difference. Your piano teacher will be able to give you a recommendation for a good tuner.

# Consider where you put your piano.

Piano placement is important. The distance of the bench from the keyboard needs to be correct, so make sure there is enough space in and around the area where you place your piano. Keeping your upright piano against an inside wall is better than having it on an outside wall. It will stay tuned longer.

Quiet time is best for practice.

Another thing to keep in mind when placing a piano in a home is not having practice time competing with family television time. It's quite difficult to concentrate on all the things a student needs to concentrate on when the TV is blaring. Imagine trying to master *Moonlight Sonata* with the ding-ding-ding of *Wheel of Fortune* going on in the background!

Make sure your child is comfortable.

Young students don't necessarily like to be tucked away by themselves when they practice. One of my students wasn't practicing very much and she finally confessed that she didn't like to practice because, "going down to the basement was scary." If that's the only option, parents should try to at least be in the general vicinity while the student is practicing.

Lighting is important to eye health.

If parents want to maintain healthy eyesight for their piano-playing student, good light should be provided at the piano. Even if there is an overhead light in the room, or a lamp near the piano, purchasing a light designated as a piano light is extremely important. Make sure to keep extra bulbs on hand.

Posture at the piano is paramount.

Posture at the piano is critical to successful practice and performance. Having the piano bench at the right height and the correct distance from the keys can enhance playing and help prevent injuries. Several of my students sit too close to the keys when they come to lessons and it's because they sit too close at home when they practice.

30

Make the bench your practice throne.

If your piano bench is not adjustable, be creative in using gym mats, pillows or carpet samples to increase height. According to Teresa Dybvig, Doctor of Music Arts, "The best height is one which both allows the elbow/upper arm to fall freely from the shoulder and allows the forearm to be parallel to the floor."

Measuring distance between body and instrument

I reminded one of my long-legged students to sit farther back when she practiced. She said, "I can't. The dining room table is in the way." Every teacher has their own way of showing a student how to determine if they are at the correct distance from the keyboard. A student should not feel "bunched up." Shoulders should be relaxed, with fingers in curved position, and arms slightly forward.

"Mom, can you grab my books?"

Ideally it would be nice to keep a shelf or a basket where a student can keep her lesson books. Keeping books in a consistent, organized space eliminates spending precious practice time locating books. Also, if Mom has to quickly grab her student's books while she is racing out the door to pick up said student from school, all the books will be together and easy to grab.

I am CEO of My Business

"We make a living by what we get, but we make a life by what we give."

~ *Winston Churchill, former Prime Minister of the United Kingdom*

Turning a hobby into a business

My chosen career is that of an independent music teacher. I have taken my long-time hobby and passion and founded a small business. I am the CEO and as all CEOs know, policies and procedures must be in place to run an efficient business and a healthy work environment. The music teacher who teaches for "pocket money" may not work the same way, but parents need to know and understand the difference.

form
Making lesson tuition easy to pay

I provide a service and you pay for that service. My studio is set up as "tuition-based" and this is the direction most independent music teachers are taking today. In a nutshell, tuition is based on the ten-month school year. For ease of budgeting, I accept equal monthly payments from September to June. I ask that the tuition check arrive at the studio by the first lesson of each month.

Paycheck to paycheck like everyone else

Independent music instructors live like most of the rest of the world: paycheck to paycheck. Imagine going into your human resources office on payday, expecting to pick up your paycheck, and being told that they will have it for you next week. A student's tuition check is the teacher's paycheck. With today's technology, there are several ways to make sure that tuition is paid on time.

Auto pay is a great way.

One way to make sure the tuition check arrives to the teacher on time is to take advantage of what your bank has to offer. Most banks these days offer the luxury of automatic bill-pay, and you can set it up online. Treat music lesson tuition like you would the mortgage payment or the electric bill. Then timely payment is no longer a worry for you and your music teacher.

Consider paying in advance up front.

If you are not comfortable with automatic payments, but you really want your music teacher to be happy about being paid on time, why not pay the full tuition up front? Some teachers offer discounts for this method of payment. Or, if your teacher prefers a monthly payment instead of a check for the full year, simply write out the checks for each month of the year and give them all to the teacher at once.

38

What does your tuition pay for?

The tuition fee covers more than just the actual lesson time. Your tuition payments are prorated over an entire year's worth of activities, not just the individual lessons. For every hour enrolled in piano lessons, you are actually investing in at least two hours of the teacher's time. Tuition pays for the whole program of activities and opportunities provided by the studio to your child during the year.

Teachers are always working for students.

Quite a lot of time is spent by teachers outside the studio, doing the following: planning curriculum, acquiring music, attending meetings, workshops and conventions to improve teaching skills, listening to and evaluating music, which also may include attendance at concerts, performing organizational tasks involved with festivals, recitals, competitions and other performance events.

40

Paperless society? I don't think so!

When a student decides to participate in adjudicated festivals and/or music competitions, there is a lot of paperwork to be read and filled out. All festivals and competitions have rules that must be understood completely. Music selections need to be timed. Registration paperwork needs to be filled out, and oftentimes, so do rating sheets for adjudicators. All of this gets done outside of the student's actual lesson time.

Volunteer work is expected in associations.

When a teacher belongs to a music association or organization in order for her students to participate in festivals, adjudications, and scholarship and award opportunities, the expectation from the association is to "give back" in volunteer time. I currently belong to three different music associations, all of which I joined for the benefit of my students. You can imagine the hours of volunteer work that is expected!

Administrative and operating costs add up.

I am reminded every year as I do my taxes that close to 45 percent of the money coming in from tuition goes out for expenses. Examples of these costs are printing, piano tuning, recital programs and treats, certificates, association dues, music magazine subscriptions, and normal operating expenses that any small business incurs. Don't forget all the music purchased for students, some of which is not reimbursed.

Cost of living raise is normal.

The cost of living and the cost of doing business both increase each year. Who gives an independent music teacher a cost-of-living raise? Families should expect a yearly tuition increase appropriate to cost-of-living increases, expenses, and services offered. I believe that most families would prefer a small, yearly increase in tuition rather than a large increase every other year or so.

Practice Guidelines that have Proven Successful

"If I don't practice the way I should, I won't play the way that I know I can."

~ Ivan Lendl, professional tennis player and coach

What does it mean to practice?

When a student has not practiced during the week, I often have the student practice during his lesson time. To turn this session into an actual lesson, I listen to how he is practicing and work with him on better practice techniques. It is a really good time to teach a student what it means to "practice" and not just play. Playing and practicing are two different things.

Consistency is the key to learning.

When you are trying to learn a new skill, don't you find it easier to keep the skill progressing the more often you practice? Consistency is the key for learning and retaining knowledge. If a student practices on Monday but doesn't touch the instrument again until Thursday, something is lost. Parents can be a huge help by providing the time, on a daily basis, when good practice can take place.

No gym needed for muscle memory.

When something is practiced over and over and over, the muscles begin to memorize what they are supposed to do, and how they are supposed to move. The great Sam Snead, professional golf player, once stated, "Practice puts brains in your muscles." Muscle memory will come naturally with practice, but never forget that intellect and imagination are also parts of the learning process.

The assignment book serves a function.

An assignment book is where the teacher writes down the assignment she'd like the student to work on and accomplish during the week, before the next lesson. If parents are ever unsure about what their child is supposed to be practicing, the assignment book is where to look. A spiral notebook is great to use. It is important for the student to bring this each week to their lesson.

Stay on task with practice log.

One way to help a student stay on task with practicing is to have them keep a practice log for keeping track of each day and the number of minutes practiced that day. Students learn to show accountability by signing the log. I also ask parents to sign the log. It really helps some students to visually see how much practice they are, or are not, accomplishing.

Don't expect perfection. Do expect progress.

It's one thing to have realistic expectations of a music student and quite another to expect perfection, especially with a beginning student. I believe in setting specific goals towards progression, based on each individual student.

Mistakes--part of the learning process

It's okay to make mistakes. They are a part of the learning process. If you have a good ear and hear your child continually playing the wrong note, don't fix it for them. Ask, "Are you sure that's the correct note?" Asking a student to figure out that note by themselves is better than doing it for them.

Parents, these are not your lessons.

Parents who do too much for their kids aren't helping. I prefer that my students learn to read music rather than hear how their parents play it and then repeat it by ear. I would like to know that my students understand the theory assignment because they completed it on their own instead of mom or dad giving them the answers.

Saying "I can't help" doesn't help.

The parent who says, "I don't know anything about music so I won't be of any help," is doing her child a disservice. Be involved, just not over-involved. Help your student understand the directions and the assignment. Consider sitting in on a lesson or two (with teacher permission). Let your child know you are invested in the process.

Encouragement is an important learning principle.

Be encouraging. Novelist Fredrik Backman said, "A simple truth, repeated as often as it is ignored, is that if you tell a child it can do absolutely anything, or that it can't do anything at all, you will in all likelihood be proven right." Encouragement at home goes a long way toward successful lessons and learning. Create opportunities for performance and applause.

Want to Please Your Teacher? Practice!

"Natural ability is important, but you can go far without it if you have the focus, drive, desire and positive attitude."

~ Kirsten Sweetland, professional triathlete

Practice "practice tips" for better practice.

I have yet to hear these words uttered in my studio: "I have too much time on my hands. I need more to practice." Students are often overwhelmed at the number of things they are being asked to do. When they have free time they usually want to play or sleep. The following lessons are practice tips designed to guide students through the practice process.

Set a scheduled time to practice.

Now, more than ever, a student must learn to be organized with her time. Schedule practice sessions each day, and do it a week in advance. Older students should have an idea of when their brains are most productive and their practice can be the most concentrated. Parents will be able to help younger students find a time that works best.

One goal focus at a time

If a student has the desire and the focus, serious progress can be made. Focus takes a lot of brain power, so focusing on one goal at a time when learning will help diminish burnout. Set goals with your teacher at each lesson as to what you and she want to accomplish. Work at accomplishing smaller, stepping-stone goals to achieve the ultimate goal.

Attention span struggles? Break up practice.

For students who have a difficult time concentrating and sitting still for very long (younger students), a practice session can be broken up. Maybe your seven-year old has a limited attention span and ten minutes is all he can handle at a time, but his teacher requires twenty to thirty minutes of practice. Break the practice time into two ten-plus minute sessions for better productivity.

Good things come in small packages.

Try practicing small sections. If your teacher writes in your assignment book to "Learn section A," but section A is a huge project for you, instead of being discouraged and turning away from practice, find a small section to work on. Look for natural breaks, or learn a phrase at a time. Beginner pieces are usually divided nicely into four-measure chunks.

Mix it up.
Learn last first.

Learning the end of a piece might prove a creative way to practice and get a student through the doldrums of practicing the same way all the time. Take the last section and learn it first, or maybe the middle section. If there are difficult passages in a piece, learn those first, even if they are completely out of order. Mix it up.

Repetitive practice produces fluency and flair.

Try different techniques for getting past the difficult sections or eliminating pauses during transitions. One technique is to play until you make a mistake, then go back to the starting point and see if you can play to get past the place where the mistake was made. Keep going back and do it over and over again until you can do it fluently, with no mistakes.

How to practice a "black page"

An experience I've had on more than one occasion is handing a piece to an intermediate-to-advanced student and having him freak out because, "The page is all black!" meaning too many notes. Students, ask your teacher to copy just two lines of the piece, from anywhere in the music, and ask to learn just that much so as to not be overwhelmed with the whole piece.

Practice log to stay goal-focused

Keeping a practice journal or practice log is a great way to stay focused on your practice goals. Don't just keep track of the days and minutes you practice, but jot down notes on what you have accomplished and what you still feel needs some work. Put your journal or log where you can see it often. It's a good reminder to practice!

63

Miraculous motto: "Practice slow, learn fast."

Slow motion! Your brain cannot take in all the detailed music information you want it to when you are playing too fast. "Practice slow, learn fast" is a great motto to remember. Only when you are very comfortable with the notes, fingering, counts, dynamics, and phrasing, should you increase the speed. Young children are at the mercy of brain development, so take it slow!

Practice piano away from the piano.

Before trying to learn a difficult piece, try studying away from the piano. Listen to a recording of the piece and make notes in your music. Look for patterns and repeated sections. Ask yourself some questions, like, "What is the composer trying to say?" Learning tricky fingering passages in a piano piece can be done at a desk or table.

65

It's not just about the notes.

Anybody can learn notes and counts (and you should certainly learn those first) but those who can make beautiful music spend extra time on understanding a piece. Learn about the composer and the time period in which it was composed, and see if you can discover the back story to the composition. Highlight the dynamics and don't be afraid to add a few of your own.

Overcoming Challenges Presented in Music Lessons

"Creating a close connection to those you do business with has its many risks, rewards, and consequences."

~ *Mark Cuban, businessman, author, and inventor*

Teachers have the right to refuse service.

It isn't easy for a teacher to release a student from her studio, but there are some good reasons that she might just do it. A termination policy should be included in the studio policies and procedures and it would be wise to address the termination policies during the interview process. We teachers do not take this lightly, so please take the time to read the policy on termination.

67

Not quite like peas and carrots

Sometimes a personality mismatch may be discovered after the initial interview process, which might be cause for release from the studio. Maybe that student will blossom under the care of a different teacher with different teaching techniques. As a teacher, I don't want a conflict with my teaching style or personality to halt learning.

Alert teacher about possible behavior problems.

If a child has behavioral problems at home or school, those problems should be discussed during the interview process. These issues could lead to a negative attitude can consist of blatant disregard for the assigned lesson (choosing NOT to do something just because they don't want to), disrespectful communication, or any type of verbal or physical abuse.

When a probation period is needed

If a student is not practicing and consistently comes to his lessons unprepared, I institute a probation period. I ask him to keep a concise practice log of days and time practiced over a certain time period. The student and a parent must sign the practice log. This gets the parent involved in the process. After the probation period, the student's situation is reevaluated.

Tardiness throws the whole schedule off.

Having a student arrive late to her lesson can cause havoc with the schedule. If your student has a thirty-minute lesson and she is ten minutes late, she will only receive a twenty-minute lesson. Parents also need to be mindful about picking up their student on time. It is not fair to ask the teacher to stay late or be accountable for that student outside of lesson time. Also, arriving too early for a lesson is not advised.

Those germs on instruments are nasty.

Please do not send a student to lessons who has a contagious cold or illness. Germs spread quickly in a music studio. If a student is sneezing and coughing but is not deemed contagious, please be aware that playing the instrument may be difficult as a student cannot keep his hands on the instrument while covering his mouth.

Teacher-hopping does not help students.

This is where the interview process shows its critical importance. It is not helpful at all to the student if she changes teachers often. Every teacher has a different teaching style and it can be confusing to a student. If you need to change for valid reasons, do so, but teacher-hopping for the sake of trying to get "the best" teacher (according to your sister-in-law) becomes a challenge to the student.

Lights! Camera! Action! Pursue Performance Opportunities

"One of the things I love about music is live performance."

~ Yo-Yo Ma, professional cellist

Is your child ready to perform?

Many parents can hardly wait for their child to appear on stage for her first performance. Most music studios have at least one recital each year, and many studios register their students in some sort of festival or adjudications. During the interview process, ask the teacher how she involves her students in performance events. Participating in performances teaches students how to negotiate and conquer nervousness and fear.

Festivals are a great starting point.

Festivals are generally considered non-competitive, but that's not always true, so do your research. The National Federation of Music Clubs is a music organization that offers an annual festival for members. These festivals are non-competitive, adjudicated performance opportunities where students earn points toward trophies. It's nice for students to get feedback from someone other than their teacher and this type of festival is great for that feedback.

Set a goal for adjudication experience.

Adjudications can be non-competitive or competitive, depending on the organization and event. Sometimes an adjudicated (judged) event can be designed so that the winner receives a place at an honors recital and/or a monetary or trophy award. The Music Teachers National Association holds annual adjudications in which students are given great feedback from a professional adjudicator.

Not for the easily stressed student

Competitions are just that--students compete against each other for some sort of prize, which could be a monetary award or simply bragging rights. Some competitions offer scholarships. Competitions tend to be a bit more stressful than adjudications and festivals, so teachers and parents need to make sure their student can handle the extra pressure.

Opportunity to strut your music stuff

Recitals are usually performed on a studio basis, meaning it's a performance event for the students in a particular studio, although studios can combine to present a recital. Some recitals have themes and students prepare selections based on the themes. Recitals are strictly opportunities to perform, and can be held throughout the year, oftentimes with a focus around the holidays or at the end of the teaching year.

Take advantage of what school offers.

Schools also offer performance opportunities. Middle schools and high schools hold annual District Solo & Ensemble Festivals where students perform in front of a judge and the judge has time to work one-on-one with the students, and provides written comments. At the high school level, students are working to place first in their division in order to advance to the State Solo & Ensemble Festival.

Talent show and family reunion performances

Family, church and school talent shows are great venues for performances. Holding a family recital when grandparents are in town is a fun time for young students to work through performance nerves. School talent shows and church programs are also fabulous venues for kids to perform. Take any opportunity for your student to perform. The more performing a person does, the less nervous he becomes.

Practice and socialize at music camp.

Music camps are intensive programs, usually lasting at least one week, where students are immersed in their instrument, possibly studying with more than one professional teacher. Most camps culminate in a wonderful recital, showcasing at least one piece a student has accomplished during camp. Camps are also a great place for musicians to socialize and share repertoire ideas.

Create special moments for the community.

Another valuable venue for performance also provides community service. Check out senior community living centers, nursing homes, rehabilitation facilities, and retirement homes and see if they would be interested in having a concert in their common area. A great recital theme for these types of groups is the celebration of Veteran's Day. Many residents enjoy singing along to tunes from their era.

How Parents can be Super Supportive

"Children learn to smile from their parents."

~ Shinichi Suzuki, inventor of the Suzuki method of music education.

Expose students to lots of music.

Parents can provide an atmosphere of music by playing different types and styles of music at home and in the car. It's hard for a teacher to know a student's musical tastes if he is not exposed to different genres. If you have access to musical theatre, the symphony, or concert events in your city, take advantage of those opportunities. Exposure is key!

Information is made available. Please read!

Teachers use various methods to get information out to parents of all students, such as a studio or teacher website, blog, Facebook page, e-newsletter, or group email. It is very important for parents to read the information they are sent. If the teacher takes the time to keep you updated, and you pay for the teacher's time, it makes sense to read what is being sent to you. Your student might believe you don't care if you don't know what's going on.

Become friends with your music store.

A good relationship with the personnel at the local music store goes a long way in obtaining printed music and all other things related to music. Your teacher probably has a very close working relationship with the music store personnel, so when you do pay a visit to your local store, be sure to mention the teacher's name. You might even get a discount!

85

Tech talk for the music student

Technology is being used more and more in music studios these days. Be aware of what your teacher uses as her teaching tools, whether it be *Piano Maestro* on the iPad, *Finale* composing software on her computer, theory game apps, or a variety of many other tech tools for teaching. Be supportive by supplying your student with access to these tools at home.

Parent time and effort is necessary.

Make the time to check in with your child every so often to see how things are progressing. Ask if you can listen to a piece she is learning. Take a look at the assignment book and ask questions. Have your child teach you something. Attend their performances and bring the grandparents along. Be supportive without being a stage parent, and above all else, don't embarrass!

Parent-teacher conference for music lessons

Ask your child's teacher for a parent-teacher conference at least once a year. This will give you the opportunity to discuss your child's progress, attitude, behavior, and skills one-on-one with the teacher. Ask if there is anything you can do at home to help. Consider your music teacher as a part of your "village" and keep them informed of anything you think she needs to know to be supportive of your child.

Provide guidance and comfort when needed.

Help your student manage time, priorities and resources. No doubt your student has other activities that demand much of her time. Make time each week to talk to your student about her schedule and when she feels overwhelmed, help her with adjustments and provide comfort as she learns about making sacrifices. Guide her through the struggles of the schedule and support her in her efforts.

Vacation education is fun and beneficial.

Summertime is a great time to take music lessons, whether private, group, or a focused music camp. Less stress of homework provides opportunities to play for enjoyment or to get ahead in music studies. Summer is also a great time for a teacher to try new music theory games or dive into some music history. Field trips to a concert or a music store are also great summer activities for musicians.

90

Motivation beefed up with incentive programs

Many teachers offer incentives to encourage students to try a little harder and accomplish a little more. Incentives don't have to be exclusive to the music studio. Parents can devise incentive programs at home to help their child continue to work on their goals such as practicing. Sticker charts work great for little kids; gift cards and money work for older kids.

Words of Wisdom to the Teacher

"It is the supreme art of the teacher to awaken joy in creative expression and knowledge."

~ *Albert Einstein*

Being more than just a teacher

We, as teachers, are asked to be more than just teachers sometimes. We are often called upon to be a different kind of listening ear. Many students are overwhelmed and there isn't always a solution to the situation. This is the time to let them know they are loved and worthwhile, that their thoughts and opinions matter. Sometimes students just need to "vent" in a safe environment.

Helping students prepare for the future

Teachers have opportunities to teach life skills, not just notes and rhythm. When a student isn't practicing, take the time to teach her time-management skills. When she is overwhelmed, give her some advice about life balance and resource (energy) management. Goal-setting is an easy skill to teach during music lessons, as is accountability. Relate these skills to the real world and help your student see how learning these skills now is beneficial to her future.

Protecting both student and teacher time

Teachers, put firm policies in place and then abide by them, to protect your business, your family, and your personal life. Those policies should also let parents know that you are protecting their student's lesson time and all that helps a teacher help a student. Review the policies annually and determine if you need to be flexible or more exacting. Consider parents' advice and ideas.

Could the problem really be mine?

When having difficulties with a student, before you think that the student has the problem, make sure you examine your behavior and expectations before blaming the student. Maybe you are asking way too much of a student because another student at his level is succeeding. Monitoring teacher expectations can help eliminate possible contention and behavior issues.

Achieving when the bar is high

I have always believed that if you set the bar high a student will reach it. I have seen it proven time and time again. But how that bar is reached is unique from student to student. Not all will reach it at the same time nor in the same manner. Because I have high expectations of my students, I have higher expectations of myself in order to help them feel and be successful.

96

Stuck in a rut? Get out!

Sometimes it's easy for a teacher to get stuck in a rut and use the same methods and tests to determine progress and success. Teachers, think outside the box. If a student wants to play a piece that is above their level (think *Clair de Lune*, *Fur Elise*, *Moonlight Sonata*), look for an abridged version and add it to her repertoire. Teachers would be wise not to measure success based only on method books and theory tests.

Good rule: authentic praise before criticism

A rule worth remembering is to praise before criticizing. Make sure your praise is authentic. Don't immediately jump on the fact that the student just missed every flat in the piece when their counting was awesome. Praise the rhythm, then ask leading questions to help them discover what they missed. Try not to follow your praise with the word "but."

Keep a healthy perspective on activities.

It's hard for a teacher not to want their wonderful students to be involved in as much as possible, such as festivals, competitions and recitals. But is it always in the best interest of the student? A teacher needs to ask herself, "What's the end game here? Pushing a student to perform or having him love music the rest of his life?" Sometimes, you just have let it be okay for a student to simply play for his own enjoyment.

Setting a positive tone in studio.

"I'm sorry that happened" is a good phrase to remember when dealing with issues either with a student or her parents. It's important for a teacher to admit when she has made a mistake, but should not take the blame if it is not hers to take. Teachers should work at keeping relationships in good standing and not take too much personally. Set a positive tone regardless.

100

Teachers, fill your glass full first.

Teachers have nothing to give if they are exhausted, hungry, frustrated or angry. Put the oxygen mask on yourself first before helping someone else. This is why sticking with firm studio policies is key. It helps you and your students respect your personal life. Get enough rest, don't skip meals because of your work, and resolve any unresolved issues as best you can. Be your best for your students.

Citations

Teresa Dybvig, teacher - *TeresaDybvig.com, WellBalancedPianist.com*

Mark Cuban, entrepreneur – *MarkCubanCompanies.com*

Fredrik Backman, author of *Bear Town*, Simon & Schuster, 2017

Winston Churchill, Albert Einstein, *A League of Their Own*, Ivan Lendl, Yo-Yo Ma, Shinichi Suzuki, Kirsten Sweetland, William Arthur Ward quotes found on *BrainyQuotes.com*

Resources

National Federation of Music Clubs – *NFMC-music.org*

Music Teachers National Association – *MTNA.org*

National Association of Teachers of Singers – *NATS.org*

Wendy Stevens, teacher and composer website – *ComposeCreate.com*

Find *Student Information*, *Enrollment Contract* and *Practice Log* forms at *SallyPalmer.com*

About the Six-Word Lessons Series

Legend has it that Ernest Hemingway was challenged to write a story using only six words. He responded with the story, "For sale: baby shoes, never worn." The story tickles the imagination. Why were the shoes never worn? The answers are left up to the reader's imagination.

This style of writing has a number of aliases: postcard fiction, flash fiction, and micro fiction. Lonnie Pacelli was introduced to this concept in 2009 by a friend, and started thinking about how this extreme brevity could apply to today's communication culture of text messages, tweets and Facebook posts. He wrote the first book, *Six-Word Lessons for Project Managers*, then started helping other authors write and publish their own books in the series.

The books all have six-word chapters with six-word lesson titles, each followed by a one-page description. They can be written by entrepreneurs who want to promote their businesses, or anyone with a message to share.

See the entire *Six-Word Lessons Series* at 6wordlessons.com

www.ingramcontent.com/pod-product-compliance
Lightning Source LLC
Chambersburg PA
CBHW070643050426
42451CB00008B/280